THE COVID-19 PANDEMIC

LIFE DURING COVID-19

by Lynn Ternus

BrightPoint Press

San Diego, CA

BrightP◇int Press

LIBRARY OF CONGRESS CATALOGING-IN-PUBLICATION DATA

Names: Ternus, Lynn, author.
Title: Life during COVID-19 / by Lynn Ternus.
Description: San Diego, CA : BrightPoint Press, [2021] | Series: The COVID-19 pandemic |
    Includes bibliographical references and index. | Audience: Grades 7-9
Identifiers: LCCN 2020050564 (print) | LCCN 2020050565 (eBook) | ISBN 9781678200602
    (hardcover) | ISBN 9781678200619 (eBook)
Subjects: LCSH: COVID-19 (Disease)--Juvenile literature. | Epidemiology--Juvenile literature.
Classification: LCC RA644.C67 T47 2021 (print) | LCC RA644.C67 (eBook) | DDC
    614.5/92414--dc23
LC record available at https://lccn.loc.gov/2020050564
LC eBook record available at https://lccn.loc.gov/2020050565

AT A GLANCE

- Starting in late 2019, a virus spread across the globe. It caused an illness called COVID-19. By mid-December 2020, the virus had killed more than 1.5 million people.

- The US government wanted to protect people from the disease. State and city leaders took action. They made rules about wearing masks. They told people to stay a certain distance away from others.

- Some leaders told certain businesses to temporarily shut down. They closed schools and asked people to stay at home. These things helped slow the disease's spread. But people's daily lives changed.

- Some people were angry with their state governments. They didn't like the new rules. They felt like their freedoms were being taken away.

- Many people in the United States lost their jobs because of the COVID-19 pandemic.

- The US economy suffered when businesses shut down and unemployment rose. Government leaders passed laws to help people and businesses. They gave money to people. It could help them pay for things such as rent and food. Leaders gave additional money to people who lost their jobs. They loaned money to businesses.

LIFE DURING A PANDEMIC

Sarah parked outside of a grocery store. She reached into her purse. She grabbed a face mask. Sarah strapped it around her nose and mouth. At the front of the store, a worker was **sanitizing** shopping carts. He wore a mask too.

Near the entrance, the floor had stickers. They read, "Please practice social

Workers at some stores cleaned shopping carts between uses to protect customers.

distancing." The stickers were placed 6 feet

(1.8 m) apart. This showed people what a

safe distance looks like. Everyone in the

store wore masks. Sometimes it was hard

to stay away from the other shoppers. The aisles were busy. People reached over to grab food right in front of Sarah. She went to check out. A plastic shield separated her from the clerk. Everyone was used to these practices. It had been this way for months.

Sarah is a fictional character. But she represents the experiences of millions of Americans during the COVID-19 **pandemic**. There were many new rules. The rules were attempts to keep people from getting the illness. Across the United States, people had to change their lives to fit this new reality.

Many businesses installed plastic shields to help protect their employees from potentially sick customers.

COVID-19 AND DAILY LIFE

In December 2019, people in Wuhan,

China, were getting sick. They had a virus.

Scientists had never seen it before. It

caused an illness later named COVID-19.

Some people with the virus had mild

symptoms. But others had chest pains. Some people had trouble breathing.

Soon, the virus was spreading across the globe. Dr. Anthony Fauci was the director of the US National Institute of Allergy and Infectious Diseases. He made recommendations to help slow the spread of the virus. Many state leaders put **restrictions** on what people could do. They asked people to stay at home as much as possible. Large gatherings were banned. Schools and businesses closed. People lost their jobs. It appeared as though everyone's lives would change.

Dr. Anthony Fauci was a member of the White House Coronavirus Task Force.

Even with these measures, the disease kept spreading. By mid-December 2020, more than 284,000 had died in the United States. More than 1.5 million had died around the globe.

CHAPTER ONE

HOW DID PEOPLE SLOW THE SPREAD?

At first, people did not know how COVID-19 spread. Experts thought people would mainly get it by touching a sick person or an object with the virus on it. Then, if people touched their faces with their contaminated hands, they could get

People washed and sanitized their hands more frequently when in public during the pandemic.

COVID-19. People washed their hands

carefully. They cleaned surfaces well.

Experts first said healthy people should

not wear masks. They said masks were

only useful to people who had COVID-19

symptoms and to health professionals

who were taking care of sick people.

They worried that if a lot of people started

buying medical masks, there wouldn't be

enough for health care workers. But experts

learned more about the virus. They learned

that the virus spreads mostly through the

air. Wearing masks can keep infected

people from spreading the disease. They

realized that wearing masks was important

for everyone.

One way the virus spreads is through

respiratory droplets. People release

these droplets when they talk, breathe,

Social distancing and wearing masks were two ways people could reduce the risk of getting COVID-19.

sneeze, or cough. These droplets can

float in the air. The virus can spread when

a healthy person breathes in the droplets

with the virus. Then he or she might get

sick. However, many of these droplets

don't spread very far. Experts said people should stay at least 6 feet (1.8 m) away from each other. That helped slow the disease's spread. This practice is called social distancing.

Masks helped keep sick people from spreading the virus. Scientists also thought masks helped keep healthy people from breathing in the droplets. In July 2020, the Centers for Disease Control and Prevention (CDC) said wearing masks was important.

TELLING PEOPLE TO WEAR MASKS

By July 2020, more than twenty states had rules about masks. Government leaders

Many states required that people wear masks in stores and at certain gatherings.

wanted people to wear masks in public.

By that time, around 130,000 people had

died from COVID-19 in the United States.

People hoped that wearing masks would

reduce the number of future deaths. Maine

governor Janet Mills wanted people in her

state to wear them. "This simple gesture is a small price to pay for knowing you could save someone's life," she said.[1]

Most people agreed to wear masks. But some people didn't want to. They said that they lived in a free country. They shouldn't have to do things they didn't want to do. They were angry when states told them to wear face coverings. People held protests. Some made signs that said, "No masks!"

Other people were confused. For a while, health experts had given different information about masks. In March, the CDC said people should wear masks only if they were sick. It also said individuals taking

care of sick people should wear masks. But

the CDC said no one else should. A couple

months later, the CDC said everyone should

wear masks. Experts said these guidelines

were based on the information they had at

NO SYMPTOMS

Some people who get the virus don't have symptoms. Symptoms can include fevers, coughing, and trouble breathing. People without symptoms may not know they have the virus. But they can still spread it to others. This is one reason health experts wanted everyone to wear masks and socially distance.

the time. But the change in advice made some people not trust the health experts.

A small number of people can't wear masks. These include young children and people with breathing problems. Many people were upset when others who could wear masks didn't. They knew wearing masks helped protect the people around them.

SOCIAL DISTANCING

People usually have to be near sick people to get the virus. Health experts and state leaders told people to socially distance.

Some people bumped elbows instead of shaking hands. This helped keep their hands clean.

They told people not to shake hands or give hugs.

Social distancing helped fight the virus's spread. It kept sick people away from healthy people. But it wouldn't make the virus go away. Instead, it would lower the number of people getting very sick at one time. Hospitals had a limited number of beds and equipment. It was dangerous if too many people needed to go to the hospitals at once. The hospitals wouldn't be able to help everyone.

SPORTS AND COVID-19

Some professional sports leagues canceled their seasons during the pandemic. The National Basketball Association (NBA) tried something different. In July, it sent teams to Disney World in Florida, which was closed to visitors. Players lived in hotels there. They played games in the area. Coaches, players, and staff members were separated from the outside world. This helped protect them from sick people.

THE ELDERLY

COVID-19 was especially harmful to the elderly. People over the age of sixty-five made up eight out of every ten deaths from COVID-19. Many older people live in assisted living facilities or nursing homes. It was dangerous if the virus spread in a space where many elderly people lived. It could kill many people. For example, by late May 2020 in Minnesota, residents in assisted living and nursing homes made up 81 percent of COVID-19 deaths.

Some of these places restricted visitors. That would help stop COVID-19 from getting into the buildings. Health experts encouraged people to use electronic devices to talk with family members. But isolation hurt older people's mental health.

Paul Da Veiga's mom was ninety-one years old. She lived in a nursing home in California and had **dementia**. Once COVID-19 hit, Da Veiga couldn't visit his mother anymore. "She doesn't understand why we're not there visiting her. . . . She thinks something bad has happened to us," Da Veiga said.[2] He worried his mom was depressed. She had lost around 20 to 25 pounds (9 to 11 kg) by September 2020.

Some elderly people were able to video chat with loved ones. But not all elderly people were able to use electronic devices.

She wanted to stay in bed all day. She didn't talk as much. Stories like Da Veiga's happened across the county. People wondered whether social distancing was helping or hurting older adults.

CHAPTER TWO

HOW DID GOVERNMENTS RESPOND?

As the virus first started to spread in the United States in late January 2020, the US government made a rule. It said most people trying to enter the United States from China would not be let in. The virus was first found in China. The US government worried people traveling

The borders between many countries were closed to most travelers in early 2020.

from there would bring more cases of the

disease to the United States.

In March, governments around the

world limited travel from other places too.

They knew if people traveled, the virus

would spread faster. The US government

suggested people in the United States

not leave the country. It also said citizens

outside the United States should come

home if they could.

Even with travel restrictions, the virus

spread around the world. Some US leaders

made rules about traveling between states.

In late March, Florida's governor said

people coming into the state from airports

in New Jersey, New York, and Connecticut

needed to **quarantine** for several days.

Some other states made rules like this

too. Massachusetts said all nonessential

workers coming into the state had to

quarantine. This included anyone coming into the state for a reason other than for an essential job, such as working at a hospital or delivering food.

STAY-AT-HOME ORDERS

Once COVID-19 cases started popping up in the United States, some governors issued stay-at-home orders. This meant that most people had to stay in their homes. They could leave to get important supplies, such as food or medicine. They could also leave to exercise outside. But they could not do this with people they didn't live with. If the stay-at-home order was for a whole state, the state was said to be shut down.

The goal of stay-at-home orders was to help hospitals. Experts wanted to spread out the number of sick people in hospitals at one time. That way, doctors would be able to treat everyone.

City streets that were normally crowded with people and vehicles were nearly empty during stay-at-home orders.

California was the first state with this order. It started on March 19, 2020. Other states began shutting down too. Some places, such as North Dakota, didn't have a stay-at-home order in the first few months of the pandemic. And other states, such as Wyoming, only had the order for certain areas. Across the country, many nonessential businesses had to close. These included movie theaters and hair salons. By late April 2020, about 95 percent of people in the United States were under stay-at-home orders.

REACTIONS TO THE SHUTDOWN

With so many people staying at home, fewer people got sick at one time. Researchers think that states shutting down for a month kept 10 million people from getting COVID-19 at that time. But some

Some people held protests about stay-at-home orders.

people were unhappy with the stay-at-home

orders. They said the states were violating

their freedoms. Some people gathered

on the streets. They protested. But most

people followed the stay-at-home orders.

Police officers had to enforce the orders.

They gave warnings or fines. These fines

were sometimes thousands of dollars.

Some states told people they could go to

jail if they didn't follow the orders.

MENTAL HEALTH

The COVID-19 pandemic was a stressful time for many people. Some people became anxious and depressed. Others were frustrated, angry, or bored. Some people coped with these emotions in unhealthy ways. They began abusing substances such as alcohol. Health experts were concerned. They gave advice to people on how to take care of their mental health. They suggested that people exercise or talk to a therapist. They also told people to get good sleep and eat healthful meals.

A pastor in Tampa, Florida, was arrested. He held church services when he wasn't supposed to. Hundreds of people attended. Sheriff Chad Chronister said this decision was dangerous. "[The pastor's] reckless disregard for human life put hundreds of people . . . at risk," he said.[3] Chronister added that he didn't want to stop people from practicing their religions. But he said community safety should be people's priority.

In Honolulu, Hawaii, a bar stayed open when it wasn't supposed to. Some people who went there got COVID-19 in July.

By September, the bar was still open. Police arrested some people there and shut down the bar.

Not being able to go places was hard for a lot of people. Kendall Jensen was a high school senior from Brentwood, California. Because of COVID-19, she wasn't able to visit colleges. That made it hard for her to pick one. All of her other high school activities, such as prom, were canceled. "Everything . . . we've been looking forward to has just been ripped from our fingers, and there's nothing we can do about it," Kendall said.[4]

Many students had to celebrate their graduations at home. They could not go to large ceremonies.

REOPENING STATES

In May, many states started to reopen. Researchers at the White House and the Johns Hopkins Center for Health Security had some guidelines. They said that before a state reopened, COVID-19 cases should be declining in that state for about two weeks.

The plans to reopen looked different for each state. In late April, Georgia's governor let nonessential businesses reopen. These included gyms and salons. But they had to sanitize. They also had to make sure customers were socially distancing.

When gyms reopened, equipment needed to be disinfected frequently.

Idaho's governor opened things more slowly. In May, childcare centers, religious buildings, and summer camps opened. The next month, he said more nonessential businesses could start to reopen.

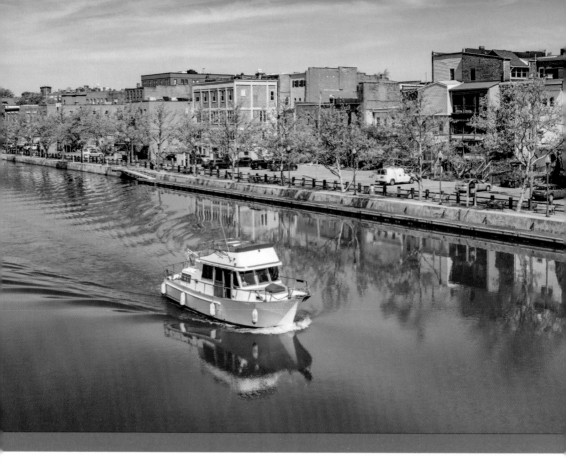

The Finger Lakes region is in the western part of New York.

New York had strict rules for reopening. That's because New York was hit hard by COVID-19. It had the most deaths in the country. More than 25,000 people had died by early May. In mid-May, the governor said only three regions of New York could open: Mohawk Valley, Finger Lakes, and Southern Tier. In these areas, manufacturing and construction projects could start. Some businesses could also do curbside pickup.

As states opened, COVID-19 cases started going up. Some states that opened quickly had a spike in cases. Others that opened more slowly had fewer cases than they did in March and April. Despite the number of cases, some people argued that the states needed to reopen. Business were suffering from the shutdowns. The economy was struggling.

CHAPTER THREE

HOW WERE BUSINESSES AFFECTED?

State shutdowns affected many nonessential businesses. Restaurants and bars weren't able to have customers inside. They lost a lot of money. Casinos had to shut down. Movie theaters closed. Other nonessential businesses included museums, malls, gyms, spas, hair salons,

State shutdowns affected small businesses the hardest. Small businesses often do not have enough money on hand to cover expenses during long closures.

and more. Each state had its own rules

about how these places could operate. In

early April 2020, forty-six states had rules

about nonessential businesses closing

for a period of time. Due to this loss of

business, some would never reopen again. In September 2020, researchers found that more than half of business closures became permanent.

Travel restrictions also hurt businesses. People didn't book flights. The airline industry suffered. Fewer people stayed in hotels. Many businesses were hit hard during the pandemic. And people working in essential businesses were affected too.

ESSENTIAL BUSINESSES

Some businesses had to stay open during the pandemic. They were essential. People working at these businesses were known

Grocery stores were essential because people always need access to food.

as essential workers. Grocery stores and

hospitals were essential businesses. Banks

and gas stations were too. States decided

which businesses were essential. Places

such as Minnesota kept day cares open.

Many people still needed childcare. Other

states, such as California, only let day cares take children of essential workers.

Essential businesses had to adjust to COVID-19. Some took employees' temperatures. They sent sick people home. Many places had new hygiene rules. Grocery stores had hand sanitizer available. They also had disinfecting wipes. People could wipe down their carts or baskets to destroy the virus. Many essential workers also had to wear masks on the job.

JOB LOSSES

Businesses struggled to survive during the pandemic. Some had to reduce employees'

Some businesses marked spots 6 feet (1.8 m) apart so customers could distance while waiting in line.

work hours or cut their pay. Others had to lay off workers. Some jobs involved seeing customers face-to-face. But this work was affected by state rules to stop COVID-19's spread. Nonessential businesses couldn't serve customers the same ways anymore. Since customers were no longer allowed inside restaurants, many restaurant workers lost their jobs. In February 2020, 6.2 million Americans didn't have jobs. By May 2020, that number jumped to 20.5 million.

Daniel Martinez was one of these people. He used to work in car repair. He lost his job in April 2020. Martinez was saving to buy a house for his family. He tried to explain to his three-year-old daughter why he didn't have a job anymore. "Some days, I feel lost and hopeless because I don't know what I can do," Martinez said.[5]

Women made up about 70 percent of servers at restaurants. Many servers lost their jobs when restaurants were not allowed to serve customers on-site.

Job losses did not affect everyone equally. More women lost their jobs during the pandemic than men. Women were more likely to work in industries that were hit hard. These included restaurants, retail, and hospitality. People of color faced similar problems. They were more likely to work in jobs that were greatly affected by the pandemic. As a result, they lost their jobs at higher rates than white people did.

THE ECONOMY

The economy is a system that rules how services and goods are made, sold, and purchased. Over time, countries' economies naturally expand and contract. Economies grow during expansion. They contract when growth slows down. Things such as employment rates and spending affect the economy.

During the 2020 pandemic, people were

not buying as many goods or services.

Businesses closed, and unemployment

rose. These things hurt the economy.

Government leaders needed to prevent

ARGUMENTS ABOUT COVID-19 AND THE ECONOMY

The economy was hurt due to the shutdowns. Most economists said that keeping things open would have led to a massive number of deaths. They thought the economy wouldn't have benefited much from keeping businesses open. But others disagreed. A few said that lots of people die from the flu every year, but states don't shut down then. However, the CDC believes between 12,000 and 61,000 people die from the flu each year. By mid-December 2020, more than 284,000 people had died from COVID-19 in the United States.

the US economy from collapsing. If an economy suddenly collapses, people suffer. There can be far-reaching hunger and homelessness. Government leaders passed laws and gave financial help to people and businesses. This gave the economy a boost.

HELPING PEOPLE AND BUSINESSES

In late March 2020, the US government passed the Coronavirus Aid, Relief, and Economic Security (CARES) Act. It included more than $2 trillion in spending. That made it the largest relief bill in US history. New York senator Chuck Schumer said,

"The legislation . . . is historic because it is meant to match a historic crisis."[6]

The CARES Act gave money to a lot of Americans. Many people got more than $1,000. They could spend the money, or they could save it. Some people used it to pay for food or rent. Other people

OTHER HELP FROM THE CARES ACT

The CARES Act helped the health care industry and local, state, and tribal governments. The act helped keep hospitals running. It gave them money for research and treatment. Money also helped them pay for important medical equipment. This included masks and ventilators. People with severe cases of COVID-19 needed ventilators to survive.

Some people used their stimulus money to shop at small businesses. This helped small businesses survive.

used it to buy goods and services. This helped the economy. The act gave more money to people who had lost their jobs. Research showed that these things helped keep about 12 million people from living in poverty.

The act also **loaned** money to businesses. The money could be used to keep paying employees. It could also cover payments on business buildings. In addition, it helped cover utility costs. This would keep businesses running.

REOPENING BUSINESSES

State leaders decided exactly when businesses reopened. The White House had guidelines. It said employers should have rules on things such as social distancing, masks, and sanitation. People with COVID-19 symptoms should not be allowed to come in to work. The White

House plan had three phases of reopening.
Each phase had fewer restrictions than the
one before. The phases depended on how
many COVID-19 cases were in the state.

Things did not immediately go back to
normal. Most businesses had to limit the
number of people inside. For example,
in late August, New Mexico restaurants
could have only 25 percent of their usual
capacity inside. Restaurants had to come
up with new ways to operate. Chaia Tacos
in Washington, DC, lost 80 percent of
its sales during the pandemic. But the
business found ways to keep running.

More people opted to have food from restaurants delivered to their homes during the pandemic.

It started delivering orders and offered takeout. Businesses and people across the nation had to find ways to cope with the pandemic.

CHAPTER FOUR

WHAT WERE WORK AND SCHOOL LIKE?

In March 2020, office work in the United States changed. Many businesses that could do so let their employees work from home full-time. This helped slow the pandemic. Working from home let people avoid crowded offices where the virus could easily spread.

Working from home helped people limit the number of other people they came in contact with. This lowered the risk of getting the virus.

In late June 2020, 42 percent of people in the United States were working from home. This lowered the number of people getting sick and dying. But people were still able to work and help keep the economy running.

Nicholas Bloom was an economist at Stanford University. He said, "Working from home is not only economically essential, it is a critical weapon in our fight against COVID-19."[7]

However, not everyone could work well from home. Some people didn't have good internet service. That is essential to being able to work from home on a computer. Other people didn't have a good office space at home. A lot of people had to work from their bedrooms or in shared spaces. Researchers found that people with more

Businesses that remained open still needed some staff, including custodians, to come into work daily.

education and higher incomes were better able to work from home.

ESSENTIAL WORKERS

In late June 2020, only 26 percent of people were going into work. Most of these people were essential workers. However, a lot of these people struggled with working during COVID-19. Their workloads increased because there were fewer overall staff. People were also scared of getting sick. And they were now responsible for enforcing safety rules in stores. Terri Prunty Kay was a Walmart cashier in California. She dealt with many angry customers each day. Some people got upset when there were limits on certain items they could buy. Others refused to wear masks. "It's been a nightmare," Kay said. She added that her work was "exhausting, mentally, emotionally and physically."[8]

Store clerks had to handle many new tasks in addition to their usual ones.

Essential workers had a higher risk for getting COVID-19 because of their jobs. Many felt underappreciated. Sabrina Hopps worked at a nursing home in Washington, DC. She was a housekeeping aide. She was responsible for cleaning rooms.

But she also spent time lifting the spirits of the elderly residents since their families couldn't visit. However, she felt like her work went unnoticed. "Housekeeping has never been respected," she said. "When you think about health care work, the first people you think about are the doctors and the nurses. They don't think about housekeeping."[9]

SCHOOLS CLOSING

In March 2020, schools across the United States closed because of COVID-19. Around 55 million students were affected. Most schools did not reopen for the rest of the school year. Instead, schools switched

MAP OF SCHOOL CLOSURES BY STATE IN SPRING 2020

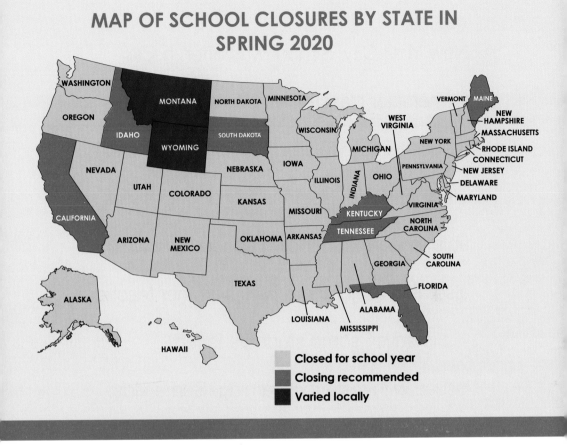

Closed for school year
Closing recommended
Varied locally

"Map: Coronavirus and School Closures in 2019–2020," Education Week, September 16, 2020. www.edweek.org.

to distance learning. Distance learning is

when teachers instruct students online.

Some students liked distance learning.

Veronique Mintz was an eighth grader in

New York City. School was often hectic for her. Her classmates would disrupt the teacher. They would also kick and hit each other. But with distance learning, she was able to learn at her own speed. She was also able to get more help from her teacher.

However, some students faced issues with distance learning. Some kids struggled with not seeing their teachers and classmates face-to-face. Others had trouble paying attention to lessons or getting motivated to learn. Some school websites crashed. Others were victims of cyberattacks.

In addition, about 12 to 15 million students didn't have access to the internet. This was a major issue since all of the learning was expected to happen online. Also, some low-income families didn't have devices for their children to use.

STUDENTS WITH SPECIAL NEEDS

School closures greatly affected students with special needs. These students often get help from different specialists at schools. Without the help from specialists, many parents worried their kids would backslide on their progress. JoAnna Van Brusselen had a daughter with mental and physical disabilities. Van Brusselen was not a special education teacher or therapist. She worried she wasn't giving her daughter the support she needed.

CHILDCARE AT HOME

Many parents struggled with balancing work and childcare with their kids home full-time. Women in particular were under a lot of pressure. The majority of moms said both childcare and household responsibilities fell to them during the pandemic. These things, on top of working full-time, created stress for many women.

Romina Pacheco was one parent who juggled childcare with work. Pacheco was always aware that her two-year-old might have temper tantrums while she was in the middle of a meeting. Caring for her kids

It was difficult for many working parents to balance their own jobs and helping their kids at home.

throughout the workday meant she often

had to work late.

REOPENING SCHOOLS

For the 2020–2021 school year, school

districts were mostly responsible for

deciding if schools should reopen. Some districts had kids go back full-time. Others continued with distance learning. Some schools had a mixture of both.

People debated about the best course of action. Kids are less likely than adults to get very sick from COVID-19. They're also less likely to die from it. Some people believed this made it OK for kids to go back to school. They reminded people that schools help kids expand their emotional and social skills. School closings can hurt children's grades. In addition, schools can be safe

As kids went back to school, they had to wear masks and distance from each other.

spaces for kids if they're being abused

at home.

However, young children could still pass

COVID-19 to adults. People working in

schools or close to children risked getting

sick. These people included teachers,

janitors, and bus drivers.

When kids started going back to school, COVID-19 cases rose. In April 2020, children made up only 2 percent of COVID-19 cases in the United States. By September, that number was 10 percent. Because the virus was spreading, some schools decided to close again.

SAFELY REOPENING SCHOOLS

Health experts had some ideas on how to safely reopen schools. They said schools should try to physically distance students. Schools should clean classrooms well, and everyone should practice good hygiene. School officials needed to keep an eye out for COVID-19 symptoms in students and staff. And everyone should wear a mask.

By late 2020, more than 1.5 million people had died from COVID-19 globally. In the United States, the pandemic affected people's daily lives in various ways. Many businesses had to close. Some people lost their jobs. Others started working from home instead of going into the office. Schools shut down for a while. In addition, people had to change their behaviors. They started wearing masks to help prevent the virus from spreading. They also socially distanced themselves from others. By doing these things, people around the country tried to slow the spread of COVID-19.

GLOSSARY

dementia

a condition where a person loses his or her memory or other brain functions

loaned

temporarily gave someone money with an agreement that the money would be paid back with interest

pandemic

an outbreak of disease that occurs over a wide area

quarantine

to isolate from others for a period of time

respiratory

related to the process of breathing

restrictions

rules that limit people in their actions

sanitizing

disinfecting something to make it clean

SOURCE NOTES

CHAPTER ONE: HOW DID PEOPLE SLOW THE SPREAD?

1. Quoted in Patty Wight, "Mills Extends State of Emergency, Strengthens Face Mask Requirements," *Maine Public*, July 8, 2020. www.mainepublic.org.

2. Quoted in Emily Paulin, "Is Extended Isolation Killing Older Adults in Long-Term Care?" *AARP*, September 3, 2020. www.aarp.org.

CHAPTER TWO: HOW DID GOVERNMENTS RESPOND?

3. Quoted in Patricia Mazzei, "Florida Pastor Arrested After Defying Virus Orders," *New York Times*, March 30, 2020. www.nytimes.com.

4. Quoted in Silvio Carrillo and Jericho Saria, "Coronavirus and the New Normal of Living in the San Francisco-Bay Area -- COVID-19 Diaries," *ABC 7 News*, April 9, 2020. https://abc7news.com.

CHAPTER THREE: HOW WERE BUSINESSES AFFECTED?

5. Quoted in Phil McCausland, "Generations of Unemployment," *NBC News*, June 30, 2020. www.nbcnews.com.

6. Quoted in Susan Davis, Claudia Grisales, and Kelsey Snell, "Senate Passes $2 Trillion Coronavirus Relief Package," *NPR*, March 25, 2020. www.npr.org.

CHAPTER FOUR: WHAT WERE WORK AND SCHOOL LIKE?

7. Quoted in May Wong, "Stanford Research Provides a Snapshot of a New Working-from-Home Economy," *Stanford*, June 29, 2020. https://news.stanford.edu.

8. Quoted in Michael Sainato, "'I Cry Before Work': US Essential Workers Burned Out amid Pandemic," *Guardian*, September 23, 2020. www.theguardian.com.

9. Quoted in Molly Kinder, "Essential but Undervalued: Millions of Health Care Workers Aren't Getting the Pay or Respect They Deserve in the COVID-19 Pandemic," *Brookings*, May 28, 2020. www.brookings.edu.

FOR FURTHER RESEARCH

BOOKS

Kerry Dinmont, *Frontline Workers During COVID-19*. San Diego, CA: BrightPoint, 2021.

Emily Hudd, *The Economic Impact of COVID-19*. Minneapolis, MN: Abdo, 2020.

Emily Sharratt, *Health Heroes: The People Who Took Care of the World*. London, UK: Simon and Schuster, 2020.

INTERNET SOURCES

"COVID-19 and the Impact on Children and Young Adults," *University Hospitals Rainbow Babies & Children*, n.d. www.uhhospitals.org.

"How to Select, Wear, and Clean Your Mask," *CDC*, October 29, 2020. www.cdc.gov.

"Outbreaks, Epidemics and Pandemics—What You Need to Know," *APIC*, n.d. https://apic.org.

WEBSITES

FEMA: Coronavirus (COVID-19) Response
www.fema.gov/disasters/coronavirus

The Federal Emergency Management Agency coordinates the federal response to national emergencies that are too large for individual states to handle, including the COVID-19 pandemic.

Johns Hopkins: The Essential Workers Project
https://bioethics.jhu.edu/research-and-outreach/covid-19
-bioethics-expert-insights/essential-workers-project

The Essential Workers Project examines how COVID-19 affected a variety of essential workers.

US Department of Health & Human Services
www.hhs.gov

The US Department of Health and Human Services (HHS) provides information about public health and safety to people in the United States.

INDEX

IMAGE CREDITS

ABOUT THE AUTHOR

Lynn Ternus is a children's book editor and author. She lives in northern Minnesota with her husband and their hyper Siberian husky puppy.